Calming Upset Customers

Staying Effective During Unpleasant Situations

Third Edition

Rebecca L. Morgan, CSP, CMC

A Crisp Fifty-Minute™ Series Book

This Fifty-Minute™ book is designed to be "read with a pencil." It is an excellent workbook for self-study as well as classroom learning. All material is copyright-protected and cannot be duplicated without permission from the publisher. *Therefore, be sure to order a copy for every training participant by contacting:*

THOMSON
™
COURSE TECHNOLOGY

1-800-442-7477 • 25 Thomson Place, Boston MA • www.courseilt.com

Calming Upset Customers

Staying Effective During Unpleasant Situations

Third Edition

Rebecca L. Morgan, CSP, CMC

CREDITS:
Senior Editor: **Debbie Woodbury**
Editor: **Luann Rouff**
Assistant Editor: **Genevieve Del Rosario**
Production Manager: **Denise Powers**
Design: **Nicole Phillips**
Production Artist: **Rich Lehl**
Cartoonist: **Ralph Mapson**

For more information contact:

    Course Technology
    25 Thomson Place
    Boston, MA 02210

Or find us on the Web at **www.courseilt.com**

For permission to use material from this text or product, submit a request online at www.thomsonrights.com.

Trademarks
Crisp Fifty-Minute Series is a trademark of Course Technology. Some of the product names and company names used in this book have been used for identification purposes only, and may be trademarks or registered trademarks of their respective manufacturers and sellers.

Disclaimer
Course Technology reserves the right to revise this publication and make changes from time to time in its content without notice.

ISBN 1-56052-669-6
Library of Congress Catalog Card Number 2002114557
Printed in Canada by Webcom Limited

5 6 7 8 PM 06 05

Learning Objectives For:

CALMING UPSET CUSTOMERS

The objectives for *Calming Upset Customers, Third Edition* are listed below. They have been developed to guide you, the reader, to the core issues covered in this book.

THE OBJECTIVES OF THIS BOOK ARE:

❑ 1) To explain the psychology that governs upset customer behavior

❑ 2) To suggest procedures to take after the customer is gone

❑ 3) To present strategies for successful customer encounters

❑ 4) To advise managers about actions and attitudes

ASSESSING YOUR PROGRESS

In addition to the learning objectives above, Course Technology has developed a Crisp Series **assessment** that covers the fundamental information presented in this book. A 25-item, multiple-choice and true/false questionnaire allows the reader to evaluate his or her comprehension of the subject matter. To buy the assessment and answer key, go to www.courseilt.com and search on the book title or via the assessment format, or call 1-800-442-7477.

Assessments should not be used in any employee selection process.

About the Author

Rebecca L. Morgan, CSP, CMC, is a people-productivity expert. She travels internationally to share her research and experience to help make people and organizations more productive and profitable. Her areas of expertise include sales, time management, communication, and creating customer service excellence.

In addition to authoring seven popular books—*Professional Selling, TurboTime: Maximizing Your Results Through Technology, Life's Lessons: Insights and Information for a Richer Life, Inspiring Others to Win, Best Practices in Customer Service, Speaking Successfully: 1001 Tips for Thriving in the Speaking Business,* and *Calming Upset Customers*—Rebecca has produced numerous audio-cassette programs, special reports, and customer service manager discussion guides. She's been featured on and in hundreds of media, including the Oprah Winfrey Show, 60 Minutes, *USA Today,* National Public Radio, *Home Office Computing,* and *Sales and Marketing Management* magazine. She has been a regular columnist for *The Customer Communicator,* and has had articles published in and/or been interviewed by *The Service Edge, First-Rate Customer Service, CRM Magazine,* and many others.

She's helped numerous companies create environments that delight customers. Her long-term solutions focus on profitability and attracting and retaining customers.

Rebecca has earned the designation of Certified Speaking Professional (CSP), which is conferred by the National Speakers Association(NSA). In 1993, when Rebecca received her CSP degree, only 214 people worldwide—less than 7% of the 3,200 NSA members—had earned this designation. She's also earned the Certified Management Consultant(CMC) designation, making her only the 15th person in the world to earn both designations.

Rebecca can be reached at:

Morgan Seminar Group

1440 Newport Avenue

San Jose, CA 95125-3329

phone: 408-998-7977

fax: 408-998-1742

http://www.RebeccaMorgan.com

e-mail: rebecca@rebeccamorgan.com

Preface

Customers make or break a business. In many businesses, upset customers are rare. But when a customer is upset, the situation can cause great stress and tension to employees and to other customers. Knowing how to resolve the conflict quickly and professionally can make a big difference in how employees perform their jobs and how customers feel about the organization.

By reading this book and completing the exercises, you will learn:

➤ Why it's important to calm upset customers

➤ Why you want customers to complain

➤ Five things you can learn from upset customers

➤ Why customers become upset

➤ What you can do to avoid customers getting upset

➤ How your words make a difference

➤ What the upset customer wants

➤ How to diffuse defensiveness

➤ What to do after the customer has left

➤ What managers need to know about calming upset customers

This third edition of *Calming Upset Customers* includes updated research data, additional examples of calming statements, and a new section devoted to calming customers via e-mail. As before, this book provides practical, easily adaptable ideas that will help you to deal effectively with upset customers in all types of situations.

Rebecca L. Morgan

Rebecca L. Morgan, CSP, CMC

Contents

A Customer Is...

The most important person to come into my organization,
whether in person, on the phone, or by e-mail or mail.

The person who ultimately pays my salary.
I really work for her.

Not someone with whom I should argue. Dale Carnegie said,
"The only way to get the best of an argument is to avoid it"
—especially with customers.

Someone with whom I will learn patience, although
he is not always patient with me.

Someone who can make or break my day,
depending upon how I react to her comments.
I can easily control my life by controlling
how I respond to situations.

Someone who has biases and prejudices just like I do.
He may not like my hair; I may not like his clothes.
Yet, he is a special human being and my customer.

Someone I take care not to offend. Even when she is wrong,
I point out the mistake indirectly and politely.

Someone who is sometimes a challenge.
I embrace the challenge and am glad
when I can turn a frown into a smile.

Someone who is very special.
She is my customer for a few short minutes
and I focus on serving her needs 100% when I am helping her.

Someone with whom I will go the "extra mile."
He may not realize it, but I realize that
the difference between mediocre and excellent is just 10%.

Introduction

> " *If you can keep your head when all about you*
> *Are losing theirs and blaming it on you...*
> *Yours is the Earth and everything that's in it."*

—Rudyard Kipling, "If"

Wouldn't it be wonderful if there were no upset customers to contend with? But that's not the way the world is. No matter how hard you try, you're bound to come across an upset person once in a while. You need to know how to respond quickly and professionally.

We have seen incidents of road rage, air rage, and general public anger escalate. C. Leslie Charles' popular book *Why Is Everyone So Cranky?* corroborates what we said in the very first edition of *Calming Upset Customers*—people are increasingly frustrated with everyday challenges, and often take out these frustrations on service personnel. This means that you have even more opportunity to hone your skills for calming upset customers! This book will help you develop those skills.

The Win/Win Solution

A recent article in *Nation's Business* quotes Doug Green, founder of New Hope Communications: "We've found that the solution to every problem comes from the spirit of cooperation. I am sure we can come up with something that can make both of us happy, but we must approach this in a very cooperative manner." This book will help you find those solutions.

"Upset" vs. "Difficult"

This book focuses on calming upset customers, who are different from *difficult* customers. When a reasonable person gets upset, she may have momentary lapses of unreasonableness, but she is still basically rational and reasonable. But difficult people have a psychological need to get attention by disruptive and negative means. They are chronically hard to communicate with.

Many of the ideas in this book will help you serve difficult people as well as upset people, but some people will be unreasonable no matter what you do. Sometimes you will have to call in your supervisor.

Customers Are Often a Challenge

You can learn from that challenge. The more you learn, the more you'll enjoy your job. Learning to calm upset people is not easy. There is no single technique that works with every upset person. But there are skills that can be learned, with a positive attitude* and practice. By the way, the ideas and skills presented in this book also work at home

Who Should Read This Book?

This book is designed to assist people who deal with the upset public to "keep their heads." The ideas presented here have been useful to people in retail, banking, insurance, medicine, utilities government, hospitality, travel, manufacturing, and other vocations. These ideas and techniques can be adapted to your job, your personal life, and your customers.

"Customers" in this book refers to clients, patients, passengers, ratepayers, insureds, taxpayers, homeowners, guests, students, patrons, or any other member of the public that you deal with who ultimately pays your salary. The concepts discussed are applicable to face-to-face interactions, telephone conversations, and even e-mail and letters.

How to Use This Book

This *Fifty-Minute™ Series Book* is a unique, user-friendly product. As you read through the material, you will quickly experience the interactive nature of the book. There are numerous exercises, real-world case studies, and examples that invite your opinion, as well as checklists, tips, and concise summaries that reinforce your understanding of the concepts presented.

A Crisp Learning *Fifty-Minute™ Book* can be used in a variety of ways. Individual self-study is one of the most common. However, many organizations use *Fifty-Minute* books for pre-study before a classroom training session. Other organizations use the books as a part of a systemwide learning program—supported by video and other media based on the content in the books. Still others work with Crisp Learning to customize the material to meet their specific needs and reflect their culture. Regardless of how it is used, we hope you will join the more than 20 million satisfied learners worldwide who have completed a *Fifty-Minute Book*.

---

*For an excellent book on this subject, read *Attitude: Your Most Priceless Possession,* by Elwood N. Chapman and Wil McKnight, Crisp Publications.

ASSESS YOURSELF

Take the following quiz to assess your skills in calming upset customers.

1 = Never	2 = Rarely	3 = Sometimes	4 = Usually	5 = Always

A. I feel I can calm most upset customers   1   2   3   4   5

B. When I'm with an upset customer, I:

➤ stay calm   1   2   3   4   5

➤ don't interrupt   1   2   3   4   5

➤ focus on his/her concern without getting
   distracted   1   2   3   4   5

➤ respond to personal accusations without
   becoming defensive   1   2   3   4   5

➤ reduce distractions of paperwork and
   telephone   1   2   3   4   5

➤ have attentive body posture   1   2   3   4   5

➤ have appropriate facial expressions   1   2   3   4   5

➤ have confident eye contact   1   2   3   4   5

➤ listen completely before responding   1   2   3   4   5

➤ take notes when appropriate   1   2   3   4   5

➤ show empathy   1   2   3   4   5

➤ let him/her know I want to help   1   2   3   4   5

CONTINUED

========CONTINUED========

➤ know when to call on my supervisor   1   2   3   4   5

➤ have a confident, helpful tone of voice   1   2   3   4   5

➤ use words that don't escalate his/her anger   1   2   3   4   5

➤ avoid blaming my fellow workers or
organization for causing the problem   1   2   3   4   5

C.   After the upset customer leaves, I:

➤ am in control of my emotions   1   2   3   4   5

➤ don't repeat the story more than once   1   2   3   4   5

➤ analyze what I did well and what I'd do
differently   1   2   3   4   5

Add up all your points to assess your score:

81–100 = Excellent

61–80 = Good

41–60 = You need to hone your skills.

21–40 = You may need to ask your supervisor for help.

1–20   = Start working with this book right now!

To make sure you have a realistic view of your skills, photocopy* the following assessment and ask your boss or co-workers to complete it, based on their observations of how you work with upset customers. If their answers are very different from yours, discuss their evaluation with them.

---

*Permission is granted to photocopy for personal use only, not for classes or other uses.

CALMING SKILLS ASSESSMENT

I'm interested in being the best I can be. Please candidly assess my skills in calming upset customers, so I can know where to focus my efforts to improve.

1 = Never	2 = Rarely	3 = Sometimes	4 = Usually	5 = Always

A. _____can calm most upset customers   1   2   3   4   5

   (name)

B. When _____is with an upset customer, I believe she/he:

      (name)

➤ stays calm   1   2   3   4   5

➤ doesn't interrupt   1   2   3   4   5

➤ focuses on concern without getting distracted   1   2   3   4   5

➤ responds to personal accusations without becoming defensive   1   2   3   4   5

➤ reduces distractions of paperwork and telephone   1   2   3   4   5

➤ has attentive body posture   1   2   3   4   5

➤ has appropriate facial expressions   1   2   3   4   5

➤ has confident eye contact   1   2   3   4   5

➤ listens completely before responding   1   2   3   4   5

➤ takes notes when appropriate   1   2   3   4   5

CONTINUED

> ➤ shows empathy   1   2   3   4   5

> ➤ lets the customer know he/she wants to
>   help   1   2   3   4   5

> ➤ knows when to call on a supervisor   1   2   3   4   5

> ➤ has a confident, helpful tone of voice   1   2   3   4   5

> ➤ uses words that don't escalate the
>   customer's anger   1   2   3   4   5

> ➤ avoids blaming fellow workers or the
>   organization for causing the problem   1   2   3   4   5

C.   After the upset customer leaves, _____
                                          (name)

> ➤ is in control of his/her emotions   1   2   3   4   5

> ➤ doesn't repeat the story more than once   1   2   3   4   5

> ➤ analyzes what was done well and what
>   needs to be done differently   1   2   3   4   5

Suggestions to help her/him become better with upset customers:

_____

_____

_____

_____

The Importance of Calming Upset Customers

2

Customer Satisfaction: Everyone's Job

In a survey of service quality conducted by the Financial Institution Marketing Association (FIMA) and Raddon Financial Group, it was discovered that 25% of customers had expressed a complaint in the previous 12 months. The survey stated, "In light of this significant percentage, everyone in the organization—from teller to president—must become increasingly aware that he or she is either serving the customer directly or is serving someone in the organization who serves the customer. All positions exist because of the customer."

Calming upset customers is rarely pleasant, but it must be done. If upset people continue expressing their anger and frustration without intervention, it can upset the whole office.

Why do you feel it's important to calm upset customers?

_____

_____

_____

_____

_____

_____

Upset Customers Don't Come Back

A recent study by e-Satisfy (formerly the Technical Assistance Research Program, a top research company on customer service issues based in Arlington, VA), showed that customer dissatisfaction is accounted for in the following ways:

➤ 20% is caused by employee actions

➤ 40% is caused by corporate products and processes that have an inherent and unwanted surprise for the customer

➤ 40% are caused by customer mistakes or incorrect expectations

Another survey showed that one out of every five supermarket customers had switched stores in the last 12 months. What made them switch? The way they were treated at the cash registers, mostly. People want and expect good service, and when they are not treated well, they don't come back.

It can be expensive for your company if your customers decide not to come back. Researchers at e-Satisfy found that the cost ratio between winning a new customer vs. retaining a current customer varies from two to one to 20 to one. That money could be spent improving your work environment, giving you a raise, or keeping you employed.

Word of Mouth Spreads Quickly

If your organization has a reputation for quick, courteous responses to complaints, people will be more apt to begin their conversation with you rationally. When customers scream and yell, it's often because that's what their friends had to do to get some action from your organization. One study found that, on average, one dissatisfied customer tells 11 other people, who each tells five others. That's 67 (1 + 11 + 55) people spreading bad word-of-mouth about your organization. Most organizations will be hurt by that much bad advertising.

A recent International Customer Service Association/e-Satisfy Benchmarking Study of Electronic Customer Service found that poor handling of online contacts created at least 30% lower customer loyalty among the two-thirds of online contacts who are not satisfied. Additionally, the study found that poor handling of online contacts resulted in a high level of negative word-of-mouth; dissatisfied online customers told twice as many people as satisfied customers (both online and off) about their experience.

You Want Customers to Complain

Yes, you do. Because if they don't complain, they'll just take their business elsewhere, and tell their friends not to do business with you. Consider what happens when you are treated poorly: do you usually complain? Most people don't. They just think, "I'm never coming here again."

A study conducted by e-Satisfy discovered that 96% of consumers do not complain to the retailer from whom they buy unsatisfactory items. This means that for every complaint the average business receives, there are possibly 24 silent unhappy customers.

Interestingly, e-Satisfy also found that, on average, for large-ticket items, 50% of customers complain to frontline employees, and 50% of complainers escalate to local management or corporate heads. The existence of an 800 number at corporate headquarters will, on average, double the number of complaints at that level. However, only one out of 100–500 will actually be addressed to a senior executive. Complaint rates vary by type of problem. Problems that result in out-of-pocket monetary loss have high complaint rates (e.g., 50–75%), whereas mistreatment, quality, and incompetence problems result in only 5–30% complaint rates to the frontline.

In addition, e-Satisfy found that customers who complain and are subsequently satisfied are up to 8% more loyal than if they had never had a problem at all.

Therefore, if a customer does complain, he or she is more likely to come back. The act of complaining can actually increase customer loyalty.

Unhappy Customer Return Rates*

No complaint: 9% (91% won't come back)

Complaint not resolved: 19% (81% won't come back)

Complaint resolved: 54% (46% won't come back)

Complaint resolved quickly: 82% (18% won't come back)

*Percentage of customers with major cause for complaint (over $100 losses) who will buy from you again.

Source: U.S. OCA/White House National Consumer Survey

In a study reported in the *Yankelovich Monitor,* 54% of adults agreed with the following statement: "It is usually a waste of time to complain to a big company when you're not satisfied with a product or service." Another study by Yankelovich Partners revealed that 90% of customers say they feel they pay enough to get the highest level of service. Yet, 64% say the service representatives they deal with don't care about their needs.

So remember: Encourage customers to complain when they have a problem. And then *do something* to help resolve the matter!

A Learning Opportunity

We can learn from every experience, if we choose to do so. A difficult encounter can be an opportunity to learn something new, or to apply what you've learned. What can you learn from dealing with upset customers?

I can learn:

_____

_____

_____

_____

_____

What You Can Learn!

Recall your worst encounter with an upset customer. You don't ever want to complain like that. Isn't anger ugly when expressed inappropriately? If you practice the following, you will become successful at preventing and calming anger in others.

> ➤ Have patience. It takes a lot of patience to listen attentively to someone while they are yelling.

> ➤ Identify specific organization procedures or practices that may be annoying to your customers. Then you can work to change these.

> ➤ Improve yourself. There may be something in your behavior that irritates people. You can work at changing this.

> ➤ Show confidence. People can tell whether you are confident in your skills. An irate person is more apt to hassle someone who appears unsure of himself.

> ➤ Learn how to calm upset people. You need to practice your calming skills.

Richard Bach, in his book *Illusions,* wrote: "You are never given a problem without a gift for you in its hands." We are given gifts in these upset people.

CALMING UPSET CUSTOMERS IN YOUR WORKPLACE

Earlier, we looked at why it is important to calm upset customers, and to actually solicit complaints from unhappy customers. Now apply these ideas to your work situation.

Why is it important for *you* to calm upset customers?

_____

_____

_____

_____

_____

Why is it important for you to encourage unhappy customers to complain?

_____

_____

_____

_____

_____

Why Customers Get Upset

Start by Looking for the Cause

Customers become upset for various reasons. Sometimes their anger is justified; sometimes it's not. Either way, in working to resolve their upset, it helps to know the cause.

Why do you think customers get upset? Write 3–5 responses in the space provided, and then compare your answers with the reasons listed on the next page.

1._____

2._____

3._____

4._____

5._____

A Customer Could Be Upset Because...

➤ She has expectations that have not been met.

➤ He was already upset at someone or something else (his boss, his spouse, his kids, a co-worker, or other business).

➤ She's tired, stressed, or frustrated.

➤ He feels like a victim—not much power in his life in general.

➤ She feels that no one will listen to her unless she yells and makes a ruckus.

➤ He will use any excuse to prove he is right, whether he is or not.

➤ She walks around with a chip on her shoulder—nothing is right in her life.

➤ You or someone in your organization was indifferent, rude, or discourteous to her.

➤ He was told one thing by one staff member and something else by another.

➤ She acted on something told to her by a staff member and it was wrong.

➤ He feels you or someone else in your organization had an unpleasant attitude toward him.

➤ She doesn't feel she was listened to.

➤ Prejudices—he may not like your hair, clothes, voice, and so on.

➤ She feels she can manipulate you to get what she wants if she makes a lot of noise.

➤ He's suspicious and thinks your organization or you are dishonest.

➤ She made a wrong assumption about what your organization would do for her.

➤ He was told he has no right to be angry.

➤ She was given a smart or flip reply.

➤ He was transferred on the phone without his consent.

➤ She was screened on the telephone.

➤ He is embarrassed about doing something incorrectly.

➤ Her integrity or honesty has been questioned.

➤ You or someone in your organization argued with him.

➤ You don't have enough job training to handle her situation quickly and accurately.

Studies suggest that the causes of customer complaints can be attributed to one of three areas: individual employees, the company, or the customer, with 80% of complaints traceable to the last two categories.

Upset People Have Little Patience

Annoyances that a person usually tolerates become intolerable when that individual is upset. You can't control another person's behavior. You can, however, change your behavior to avoid causing annoyance. Look again at the reasons why customers get upset. Which ones do you have any control over? In the space below, list those you think you can at least partially control, and briefly note what your responsibility is:

Causes I May Be Able to Control

Action I Can Take to Help

_____   _____

_____   _____

_____   _____

Avoidable Upsets

The annoyances you have some responsibility for causing include the following:

➤ **You or someone in your organization promised something that was not delivered.**

If you promised the customer you would get back to him and you didn't, then he may become upset. With good reason. Most of us become upset when people promise action and don't follow through.

➤ **You or someone in your organization was indifferent, rude, or discourteous.**

Discourtesy is often unintentional. You may not have thought about your statement before you blurted it out. Some people try to make funny comments, but these may come across as rude. Treat every customer as you would a special guest or relative.

➤ **The customer feels you or someone else in your organization displayed an unpleasant attitude toward him.**

Perhaps this customer was surly himself, dressed unusually, or treated you poorly. This is no excuse for you to react unprofessionally.

Straighten Up and Fly Right!

While I was waiting in the airline check-in line, the ticket agent announced, "The line in front of me is for passengers checking in for Flight 64. The line to the right is for the problems."

➤ **She doesn't feel she was listened to.**

People want to be listened to. They don't want to have to repeat themselves.

➤ **He was told he has no right to be angry.**

Everyone has a right to his or her emotions. Telling a person otherwise is sure to make him or her even angrier.

➤ **She was given a smart or flip reply.**

Sarcastic remarks only heighten anger, they seldom ease it.

➤ **He is embarrassed about doing something incorrectly.**

Make sure the customer understands what he needs to know before he tries to use your product or service. Go over any procedures about returns or guarantees beforehand. That way, you'll have fewer customers who are angry because of a misunderstanding.

➤ **Her integrity or honesty has been questioned.**

Treat customers with respect and dignity. If there is a problem, assume your organization has made the mistake until shown otherwise. Instead of saying, "You didn't pay us," say, "We don't have a record of receiving your payment. Would you be kind enough to see if your check has cleared the bank?"

Work to eliminate body language, voice tone, or facial expressions that convey distrust. Avoid projecting an "us versus them" attitude about customers.

Never call a customer a deadbeat, liar, cheat, thief, etc. Never threaten a customer.

Angel of Mercy?

At 5:00 the nurse calls my name. As she's showing me to the examination room, I comment, "The doctor must be very busy today. I arrived at 4:05 for my 4:10 appointment." She responds, "I checked the waiting room for patients an hour ago. You must have been late for your appointment."

➤ **You or someone in your organization argued with the customer.**

As Dale Carnegie said: "The only way to get the best of an argument is to avoid it." This is especially true with customers. If you argue with a customer, you always lose—even if you win the argument. It's not good for other customers to witness an argument. They won't like seeing you treat a customer poorly, whether or not the customer was in the wrong.

Returning Calls

Following up on the information you promised is one way you can avoid upsetting callers or visitors. Even if you have to call a customer back to say you're still checking, she'll appreciate knowing that you haven't forgotten and are doing your best.

Below is a simple form you can duplicate* to keep track of the follow-up responses you promise. If you have customers in different time zones, this will help you remember to call them back during their workday. Keep this form in front of you to remind you of what you've promised.

CALLBACK SCHEDULE

	Name	Phone #	Regarding
before 8:00			
before 9:00			
before 10:00			
before 11:00			
before 12:00			
before 1:00			
before 2:00			
before 3:00			
before 4:00			
before 5:00			

*Permission to photocopy for personal use only, not for classes or other uses.

Preventing

Behaviors That

Irritate Others

Be Proactive in Preventing Escalation

Now we will look at what you can do to avoid turning a dissatisfied customer into an angry one. By being proactive in how you present yourself to customers, you can directly influence whether a minor irritation escalates into an angry confrontation. In this section, you will learn the importance of:

➤ Personal presentation

➤ Nonverbal communication

➤ Words that make a difference

Personal Presentation

One of the things that can irritate an already upset customer is your personal presentation. If he feels your grooming and dress are unprofessional or inappropriate, he is more likely to hassle you.

Here are some areas of personal presentation that, if not seen to, may have a negative influence on an upset person.

Check to make sure that your:

➤ Hair is clean, brushed or combed, and well kept

➤ Makeup is applied neatly, moderately, and appropriately

➤ Clothing is pressed, neat, clean, and in good repair

➤ Hands and fingernails are clean

➤ Nail polish is fresh and unchipped

➤ Face is shaved or mustache/beard is neatly trimmed

➤ Stockings are run-free

➤ Breath is fresh

Can you think of anything else?

_____

_____

How can your personal presentation affect how an upset customer reacts to you?

_____

_____

_____

_____

_____

First Impressions

We all make assessments of others, and initially those assessments are based mainly on personal presentation. Some experts claim we make decisions about people within the first four seconds of meeting them.

Bay Alexander, President of Professional Impact in Corralitos, California, says:

"If you are in a position where you are likely to interact with angry customers, you have a chance to use your image as one of your more effective tools. You can use your image to signal your power, control, knowledge, and composure. If you are dressed inappropriately or too casually for your position and business, customers are more likely to push to get their way, and call for a higher authority if they don't like your response."

You may have experienced the power of your appearance when you were a customer. Have you noticed how much easier it is to return an item to a store when you are neatly dressed than when you wear torn jeans and a dirty T-shirt?

You never get a second chance to make a first impression.

Nonverbal Communication

Here are some ways your body language and voice tone may influence an upset person:

Facial Expression

When people complain, do you ever roll your eyes?

Do you scowl?

Do you have an inappropriate smile?

Be aware of your facial expression when you communicate. Ask friends, co-workers, and your supervisor whether you have facial expressions that could be annoying, especially to upset customers.

You want to have a calm, concerned, sincere, interested facial expression. Show the customer you care.

Some people smile when they are tense; don't smile when a customer is expressing anger. If you do, the customer may feel that you're not taking her seriously.

Body Posture

Do you loll about your work area?

Do you slouch?

Show you are attentive to your customer by standing and sitting up straight. When you loll or slouch you may seem inattentive or disinterested.

Maintain a nonthreatening, open body posture. Stand far enough away to give the customer room. Don't crowd him—this may increase his irritation.

Movement

Do you move slowly when you have to find something for the upset customer?

Upset customers want to see you respond to their needs quickly. This doesn't mean you have to sprint to help, but don't take your time either.

Gestures

Do you stand/sit with your arms crossed?

Do you hold your head up with your hand(s)?

The most common interpretation of the arms-crossed gesture is that the person is closed and unwilling to listen. When communicating with an upset customer, uncross your arms to show you are listening and have an open mind.

Smoking

Don't smoke in front of customers, even if your employer allows you to smoke in your work area. Always put the cigarette out, even if your customer is smoking.

Touching

Avoid touching an upset person, especially if he appears potentially violent. This could set off his violence. Touching also implies familiarity, and is inappropriate with customers, upset or not.

Chewing Gum or Eating

Don't chew gum or eat when you're on the phone or in the public eye. Even if your employer allows it, these acts can be annoying, and can change an upset customer into an irate one.

Voice Tone

Your attitude is projected through your voice as well as your body language. Remember that helping customers is your job, and if you can't stand to help upset people, get transferred to another job. Make sure your attitude is always, "I'm here to help as best I can."

Do you sound annoyed?

Does your voice go up at the end of a statement?

People respond more strongly to *how* you say something than to what you say. When your voice is annoyed, impatient, or condescending, the customer will become more angry. When your voice sounds confident, she will believe you know what you're talking about and it will be easier to calm her.

When your voice goes up at the end of a sentence, it sounds as if you're asking a question. Record and listen to your voice on a tape recorder and note whether your voice goes up at the end. If so, practice having an even tone, or one that ends on a lower note. You will sound confident and competent.

Speak with a calm, firm, caring, soothing tone.

Sighing

Sighing often suggests annoyance or impatience. Don't sigh in front of an upset customer.

Cursing

Even if the customer curses, there is never an excuse for you to curse. No matter how many insults he shouts at you, remember that you are a professional. Compose yourself as best you can, and avoid responding to abuse.

It is a sign of strength, not weakness, to stay calm and respond with patience when someone is cursing and insulting you.

In what areas do you need to improve?

I need to improve my:

- ❑ Body language
- ❑ Facial expression
- ❑ Body posture
- ❑ Movement
- ❑ Gestures
- ❑ Smoking
- ❑ Touching
- ❑ Chewing gum or eating
- ❑ Voice tone
- ❑ Sighing
- ❑ Cursing

Words That Make a Difference

The words you use with customers can help communicate or they can start a fight. Here are some common Fight Starters and some suggestions for replacing them with Communication Helpers.

Keep It Impersonal

Fight Starter: **Communication Helper:**

You didn't do this right.   *There are a few areas on this form that we need to complete.*

If the customer did something wrong, point out the mistake indirectly. She will often be embarrassed by her mistake. She may get angry because of this embarrassment and try to blame you.

Avoid statements that are sarcastic, blaming, or condescending. Even if the customer is wrong, the time to make it known is not during a rage.

Use "I" Instead of "You"

Fight Starter: **Communication Helper:**

You're wrong.   *I can see there's been a miscommunication (or misunderstanding).*

Fight Starter: **Communication Helper:**

You're confusing me.   *I'm confused.*

Don't blame the customer. When explaining what went wrong, use either the indirect approach or "I" statements as much as possible.

Avoid Giving Orders

Fight Starter: **Communication Helper:**

You have to...   *Will you...please*

                                            It would be best if we...

                                            It would be best if you...

People like to be given a choice. Ask them pleasantly to do something or explain how it will be to their benefit.

People don't like to be given orders. Rephrase it more politely as a question.

Fight Starter:	**Communication Helper:**
You should have done it this way.	*We want your next visit to go as smoothly as possible. This will assist you.*

Fight Starter:	**Communication Helper:**
Wait here.	*Would you mind waiting while I speak to my supervisor?*

When people hear "should," they often think of their parents or some other authority figure telling them what they did wrong. Instead of telling them what they should have done, tell them what will be helpful in the future. The past is past and there's nothing anyone can do about it. Focus on the future—the next time—instead.

Take Responsibility

Tell the customer what he and you can do, not what can't be done.

Fight Starter:	**Communication Helper:**
I can't...	*I don't have the authority. However, Mary should be able to help you. Let me get her.*
	You can...

If you cannot help, connect the customer with someone who can.

Fight Starter:	**Communication Helper:**
It's not my job.	*Let me see what I can do to help.*
	John is the specialist in that area. Let me get him for you.

Even if what the customer needs isn't within your job duties, never tell her that. Tell her how you can help.

If people think they're being criticized, they'll react defensively—that is, angrily.

Avoid Causing Defensiveness

Fight Starter: **Communication Helper:**

You never do it right.   *This is often not done correctly.*

You're always late.   *This payment is often late.*

"Always" and "never" sound critical and uncompromising; use "often" instead.

Fight Starter: **Communication Helper:**

You filled this out   *You filled this out well, and...*
okay, but...

People don't listen to what you say before the "but"; they concentrate on what follows. Use "and" instead, so they'll listen to the whole sentence.

Fight Starter: **Communication Helper:**

It will cost you...   *The rate is...*

"Cost" sounds negative, and costs can imply time, aggravation, and other things in addition to money.

Fight Starter: **Communication Helper:**

What's your problem?   *Please tell me what happened.*

People don't like to have problems, and they don't like others to know they have problems. Use the communication helper instead.

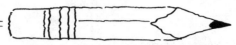

WATCH YOUR WORDS

You can see how important it is to choose the right words and show a positive, helpful attitude. How would you respond in the following situations?

1. **Customer:** *"Can you put this sweater on hold for me?"*

   Staff: *"I can only hold it until closing."*

   Why wouldn't you say this to a customer?_____

   _____

   How would you rephrase the response?_____

   _____

2. **Customer:** *"I would like to be on the preferred customer mailing list."*

   Staff: *"You have to have spent $1,000 or more."*

   Why wouldn't you say this to a customer?_____

   _____

   How would you rephrase the response?_____

   _____

3. **Customer:** *"Why haven't I received my refund?"*

   Staff: *"Because you filled in the form wrong."*

   Why wouldn't you say this to a customer?_____

   _____

   How would you rephrase the response?_____

   _____

4. **Customer:** *"Do you have mittens?"*

   Staff: *"You'll have to go to accessories for that."*

   Why wouldn't you say this to a customer?_____

   _____

   How would you rephrase the response?_____

   _____

CONTINUED

5. **Customer:**   *"Are there any more of these forms?"*

    Staff: *"I don't think so."*

    Why wouldn't you say this to a customer?_____

    _____

    How would you rephrase the response?_____

    _____

6. **Customer:**   *"How can I get hold of Dr. Jackson?"*

    Staff: *"Call her."*

    Why wouldn't you say this to a customer?_____

    _____

    How would you rephrase the response?_____

    _____

7. **Customer:**   *"I'd like to change something on that job you're doing for me."*

    Staff: *"You'll have to come to our office tomorrow. It's too late to
                    do it today."*

    Why wouldn't you say this to a customer?_____

    _____

    How would you rephrase the response?_____

    _____

8. **Customer:**   *"Why can't I get my software to run?"*

    Staff: *"Because you didn't read the manual."*

    Why wouldn't you say this to a customer?_____

    _____

    How would you rephrase the response?_____

    _____

CONTINUED

9. **Customer:**   *"I need the number for one of your branch offices."*

    Staff: *"I'm busy with a customer. Here, look it up yourself."*

    Why wouldn't you say this to a customer?_____

_____

    How would you rephrase the response?_____

_____

10. **Customer:**   *"I got a refund for $24.95 when I requested $42.59."*

    Staff: *"You must have sent in the request for $24.95; otherwise, we would have sent you the other amount."*

    Why wouldn't you say this to a customer?_____

_____

    How would you rephrase the response?_____

_____

11. **Customer:**   *"How do I get to the Shamrock Room?"*

    Staff: *"There's a map over there."*

    Why wouldn't you say this to a customer?_____

_____

    How would you rephrase the response?_____

_____

12. **Customer:**   *"Why haven't I received my order yet?"*

    Staff: *"Because I've been handling customer problems."*

    Why wouldn't you say this to a customer?_____

_____

    How would you rephrase the response?_____

_____

13. **Customer:**   *"Why do I need to show you my identification? I've been banking here for years."*

   Staff: *"It's bank policy."*

   Why wouldn't you say this to a customer?_____

   _____

   How would you rephrase the response?_____

   _____

14. **Customer:**   *"I need someone to help me with a problem on my account."*

   Staff: *"You'll have to wait for Susan to get back from lunch."*

   Why wouldn't you say this to a customer?_____

   _____

   How would you rephrase the response?_____

   _____

15. **Customer:**   *"How do I make this computer I bought from you run?"*

   Staff: *"It's in the manual."*

   Why wouldn't you say this to a customer?_____

   _____

   How would you rephrase the response?_____

   _____

16. **Customer:**   *"Would you check the status on our account?"*

   Staff: *"The computer is down. You'll have to call back tomorrow."*

   Why wouldn't you say this to a customer?_____

   _____

   How would you rephrase the response?_____

   _____

*Compare your answers with the author's suggested responses
in the back of the book.*

32

Practicing Behaviors That Calm Customers

34

Taking Action to Reverse Anger

We've discussed how your personal presentation, body language, voice tone, and choice of words can irritate customers. Once the customer is angry—for whatever reason—you need techniques for calming him down. In this section, we'll look at:

➤ What upset customers want

➤ Listening habits

➤ More words to watch

➤ Additional pointers

➤ Calming customers over the phone

➤ Calming customers via e-mail

➤ Steps for dealing with an upset customer

The Customer Wants...

➤ **To be taken seriously**

The customer does not want a response like "You're kidding," "No way," or "You've got to be joking." He wants you to be professional and confident and to respond seriously to his concern.

➤ **To be treated with respect**

The upset person doesn't want condescension or arrogance. She wants you to treat her and her concern with respect. This may be difficult when the customer is clearly at fault but is trying to blame your organization.

➤ **Immediate action**

He doesn't want you to look into it next month, next week, or even tomorrow. He wants you to do something now. Show you are concerned by moving briskly, no matter how tired you are.

➤ **Compensation/restitution**

He wants someone to pay for the damage done, and perhaps for his time, inconvenience, or pain.

➤ **Someone to be reprimanded and/or punished**

Assure the customer that corrective action will be taken, even if you aren't the supervisor. Discreetly report the incident to the supervisor so she can explain the problem to your co-worker and avoid similar problems in the future.

> ## To clear up the problem so that it never happens again

Sometimes the customer just wants to know that some action has been put in motion, so that no one will have this problem again. Assure her you will report the problem to the person who can take care of it.

> ## To be listened to

What the upset customer wants first is to be listened to. It is difficult to listen carefully in a tense situation, especially if you have not developed effective listening habits.*

Why don't we listen well? What habits do you think prevent people from listening fully, especially in stressful situations?

_____

_____

_____

---

*For an excellent book on listening, read *The Business of Listening* by Diana Bonet, Crisp Publications.

Listening Habits

According to Dr. Lyman K. Steil, president of Communication Development, in St. Paul, Minnesota, most people have poor listening habits. Some of the habits Dr. Steil has discovered include the following:

➤ **Criticizing the speaker and delivery**

This focuses not on what the speaker is saying, but how she is saying it. If you focus on a lisp, a stutter, an accent, a dialect, grammatical errors, and "ums" and "uhs," you are missing the speaker's thoughts and feelings.

➤ **Listening only for facts and not for feelings**

A customer may not say he's angry, but his voice conveys it loudly and clearly. Listen carefully for emotions as well as facts.

➤ **Not taking notes—or trying to write everything down**

Not taking notes can cause problems later, when you try to remember what was said. On the other hand, trying to take down everything the customer says will make you lose eye contact. Take a few brief notes of important details, like dates, times, amounts, and account numbers.

➤ **Faking attention**

Customers can quickly discern if you are paying attention to them or not. If a customer was mildly agitated before, your inattention will make her angry. Pay close attention when you are helping her.

➤ **Tolerating or creating distractions**

Don't be distracted by other conversations. Eliminate visual distractions by removing paper piles and pulling out a clean piece of paper to take notes. Listen fully to the customer and eliminate whatever distractions you can.

➤ **Tuning out difficult or confusing information**

When people are upset, they don't always communicate clearly. If you habitually tune out what you don't immediately understand, practice asking the person, in a pleasant manner, to slow down. It's easier to understand information one piece at a time. Take notes to help you put the pieces together.

➤ **Letting emotional words block the message**

The upset customer may call you names, curse, or say unpleasant things about you, your co-workers, and your organization. Avoid letting him "push your buttons" in this way, because when you're upset you've lost objectivity, and you need to be in control if you're going to find a solution to the situation.

➤ **Interrupting or finishing the other person's sentences**

This is an irritating habit and will only induce more anger in an already upset person.

➤ **Biases and prejudices**

We all have biases and prejudices, whether we like it or not. You may not like a person's style of dress, or hairstyle, or stutter. It is hard to listen when you're distracted by these biases. Work on eliminating your prejudices to be a better listener.

➤ **Not facing the upset person**

Look her in the eye. Remember what your parents said when you were a kid: "Look at me when I'm talking to you." People see you are listening when you are looking at them.

➤ **Not ensuring that you've understood**

Repeat what you understand the customer to be saying. Start your sentence with "Let's see if I understand..." or "I think I understand..." (and then paraphrase what she said). Don't say "What you're trying to say is..." —it implies the customer is an idiot and can't say what he means. Also avoid "What I hear you saying is..." —it's overused and trite.

More Words to Watch

In the last section, we looked at words that can be annoying and words that are more neutral—Fight Starters and Communication Helpers. Here are some more words to avoid—because they'll enrage someone who's already upset—and alternatives that help to calm the person down.

Use Verbal Cushions—Show Empathy

Verbal cushions let the customer know that you can understand why she would be upset. You're not saying you know exactly how she feels, because you can't know that.

You're also acknowledging her right to feel that way. You're not discounting her feelings.

Fight Starters:	Communication Helpers:
You're crazy.	*I can appreciate what you're saying.*
I know how you feel.	*I can understand how you'd feel that way.*
	I can understand how that would be annoying.
Boy, you're sure mad.	*I can see how you'd be upset.*
I don't know why you're so upset.	*I would be upset, too.*
	I'm sorry for your inconvenience.

Use the Three Fs: Feel, Felt, Found

The three Fs are a skeleton on which to hang the rest of your response. This technique acknowledges the customer's feelings and offers an explanation in a way she can listen to:

"I understand how you could feel that way. Others have felt that way too. And then they found, after an explanation, that this policy protected them, so it made sense."

Get Clarification

Paraphrase what he is saying. Take the blame if there is a miscommunication. Make sure you understand the concern before you try to solve it.

Fight Starters:	**Communication Helpers:**
You're way off base.	*I'm sorry, I need to better understand...*
You aren't making any sense.	*Maybe I misunderstood...*
That's definitely wrong.	*Let me see if I've got this straight...*
Did you really say...	*Here's what I understood you to say...*

Form a Team

Let her know her patronage is important. When you form a team, it is the two of you together working on a solution, rather than her vs. you.

Fight Starters:	**Communication Helpers:**
We can't do that.	*I want to help find a solution.*
You sure have a problem.	*Let's see what we can work out together.*

Additional Pointers

Take Time Out

If you find yourself becoming upset, or wanting to cry or yell at the customer, allow yourself a little time away from the situation. This will give you a chance to calm down before you address the problem.

When you know you're getting emotional, excuse yourself politely:

"Excuse me a moment while I check the policy on this."

"I'd like to get my supervisor's opinion on this."

"I need to verify some information in the file."

"I need to discuss how we can best solve this. I'll be just a moment."

Always excuse yourself in a way that shows your interest in serving the customer.

Don't Cry

Upset customers can say things that are hurtful, often without realizing that you may take their comments personally. Whatever you do, don't cry in front of the customer. If your emotions take over, you cannot be as professional as you need to be.

If you find yourself beginning to cry, excuse yourself and go to an empty office, the rest room, or a back room so you can compose yourself undisturbed. If you don't feel you can bear talking with the customer, ask one of your colleagues or your boss to take over.

Get the Customer's Attention

If the customer is ranting and not giving you a chance to explain or ask questions, use his or her name at the beginning of your sentence. Most people listen when they hear their name.

Handle the Obstinate Customer

If you are having trouble reaching an agreement, make comments that direct the customer toward finding a solution:

> *"What would you like me to do now?"*

> *"What do you think is a fair way to settle this?"*

> *"What would make you happy?"*

Often, what she will ask for is less than you might have offered. If the customer's proposal is within your guidelines, accept it. If not, make a counterproposal.

If you can't reach an agreement, it's time to call in your boss. Unless you are a manager, it is not your place to invite a customer to take her business elsewhere.

Use Polite Repetition

If the customer keeps insisting on something that's unreasonable or impossible, tell them what you can do (not what you can't do). Keep repeating it, without becoming hostile or loud, until you're finally heard. For example, if the customer insists on getting a widget, and you have none in stock, the conversation might go like this:

> *"I want my widget today."*

> *"I'm sorry, we will have more widgets in on Tuesday."*

> *"But I need it today."*

> *"I'm sorry, we don't have any in stock."*

> *"I want it today."*

> *"I'll be glad to get one to you on Tuesday."*

Eventually, you may have to ask him to leave. If he won't, call in the security guards or the police.

A Special Note on Dealing with Violence

There may be occasions when an enraged customer threatens you, or becomes violent. Rely on your gut feeling if it seems things are getting out of hand. Learn to look for potentially violent behavior by reading the nonverbal communication of the customer—clenched fists, tight lips, agitated tone of voice, tense body posture, flared nostrils, red face, and wide-open eyes. Look for evidence of drugs or alcohol.

If the customer becomes unruly, or threatens violence, seek assistance. You do not have to put up with threats.

Never try to reason with a drunk or a drug user. Even if there is no sign of drugs, if the person appears potentially violent, don't feel stupid about calling the police. There are plenty of stories about employees being punched by upset customers. It's better to risk feeling stupid than to end up in the hospital.

Never accuse a customer of being drunk or on drugs. This can put you and your company in a liable situation. Find another way to assist the customer away from your establishment.

For more information, read *Preventing Workplace Violence* by Marianne Minor, Crisp Publications.

Calming Customers Over the Phone

It is easier for a customer to be abusive on the phone because you are a faceless representation of the organization. The guidelines we've discussed throughout this book generally apply when calming customers on the phone. There are a few areas you'll need to modify, however.

Because there is no face-to-face contact, communicating over the phone presents special challenges. You only have your voice tone (e.g., inflection, pitch, and volume) and word choice to communicate your caring to the customer. It is estimated that over the phone, the listener understands your message 80% from your voice tone and 20% from your words.

You can see how critical it is that your voice tone be pleasant, concerned, patient, informed, and caring. When a customer cannot see your concerned face, she needs to hear concern in your voice. It also helps to deepen your telephone voice. Lower voices are perceived as being more mature, confident, and in control.

There are several ways to check whether you have a good voice tone. One way is to get feedback from your boss or a co-worker. It must be someone who will be honest with you, yet offer feedback caringly. Another option is to record yourself. Although your voice on tape may sound different to you than you think it should, this is an excellent way to discover how others hear you.

You could still be annoying customers, even if your voice is pleasant. You may have irritating habits, such as mumbling, gum chewing, eating, covering the receiver to talk to co-workers, or leaving the customer on hold too long.

If you need to leave the line during a call, ask the customer if she'd rather be called back or put on hold. If she prefers to be called back, tell her you'll call her by a certain time, and ask if that's acceptable. Call back at the agreed time, even if you've nothing to report except that you're still working on the problem.

If she prefers to be kept on hold, explain that it may be several minutes before you'll have the information. Give her your name in case she decides to hang up and needs to call again. And ask for her number in case you get disconnected.

This kind of service shows the customer that she really matters, and that your organization is run by thoughtful, helpful people, not cold computers.

Calming Customers Via E-mail

Just as calming an upset customer on the phone has special considerations, so does calming a customer via e-mail. It is easy to misinterpret words, tone, and intent in an e-mail. You must be extra careful to word your e-mail response to an upset customer, so your message doesn't further irritate the customer.

➤ Create boilerplate responses to the most common issues addressed via e-mail. Work with your supervisor to word these carefully so that they are friendly, and prevent the possibility of misinterpretation. However, make sure your response fits the customer's question or concern. It can be doubly annoying to receive a form response that doesn't address the question asked.

➤ Be friendly in your word choice, but not too casual.

➤ Check your message thoroughly for typos.

➤ Thank the customer for letting your organization know there is a problem, and outline your steps for rectifying it.

➤ Show concern for the customer's situation and frustration.

➤ State any additional information you need from the customer.

➤ Give the customer your direct telephone number in case she wants to talk to a live person.

➤ If you have technical notes pertaining to the inquiry, copy the text into your response, rather than just referring the customer to a Web page.

Steps for Dealing with an Upset Customer

When you're dealing with an upset customer:

STEP 1. Verbally cushion the customer's concerns.

> *"I can understand how that would be frustrating."*
>
> *"The manual can be confusing."*

STEP 2. Use the three Fs.

> *"I can understand how you could feel that way. I felt that way when I first heard our policy. So I asked my supervisor, and found out how it really protects our customers. Let me share what I learned..."*

STEP 3. Apologize for the situation.

> *"I'm sorry that no one has called you about this."*
>
> *"I apologize for your inconvenience."*

STEP 4. State that you want to help.

> *"I want to find a solution for this situation."*
>
> *"I want to resolve this for you as quickly as possible."*

STEP 5. Probe for more information.

> *"Help me understand more..."*
>
> *"Please tell me what happened."*

STEP 6. Repeat the concern to make sure you have understood.

> *"Let me see if I understand correctly..."*
>
> *"Before proceeding, I want to make sure I have all the facts right..."*

STEP 7. Show that you value the customer's patronage.

> *"We value your business and want to fix this promptly for you."*
>
> *"You are an important customer so we want to resolve this quickly for you."*

STEP 8. Explain options or ask what the customer would like to have happen.

> *"Here are three actions I can take to resolve this. Which one would you prefer?"*

> *"What do you think would be a fair way to resolve this?"*

STEP 9. Summarize actions to be taken—yours and the customer's.

> *"Mr. Garcia, as we agreed, you'll fax me a copy of the notice you received, and I'll take it immediately to my manager for resolution."*

STEP 10. End pleasantly.

> *"Ms. Fukumoto, I'm sorry this has been a hassle for you. I appreciate your bringing this to our attention so we can straighten it out immediately. Thank you for calling."*

Throughout:

- ➤ Listen

- ➤ Face the customer

- ➤ Look him/her in the eye

- ➤ Adopt a concerned body posture, voice tone, and facial expression

- ➤ Avoid Fight Starters

- ➤ Avoid a condescending or impatient tone

- ➤ Have and show empathy

- ➤ Eliminate distractions

- ➤ Practice patience

- ➤ Use a pleasant tone of voice

- ➤ Don't take things personally

A Note About Case Studies

The purpose of a case study is to provide insights you may not otherwise gain by just reading about ideas and skills. Four case studies are included in this book to present specific situations to think about and to show how you can apply important ideas and skills to real situations.

These cases do not have exact solutions or answers. Different points of view are always possible–and even encouraged–in discussions of people, their attitudes, and their behaviors. You can benefit in two ways from these case studies:

➤ By analyzing the case and expressing your views

➤ By comparing your ideas with the author's comments at the back of the book

Well yes, Madame...but we **DID** remove the stain.

THE CASE OF THE SURLY SALESPERSON

Sometimes salespeople can inadvertently *cause* an upset by the way they approach customers. That was the case in the following conversation, a portion of an actual call from a national long-distance telephone company sales representative.

Salesperson: *I'm with (national long-distance phone company) and I'm calling about your video, Calming Upset Customers. Why don't you have an 800 number?*

Rebecca: *We do have one. Tell me, where did you hear about the video?*

Salesperson: *I have an ad you placed in a magazine.*

Rebecca: *Hm. I didn't place an ad. What magazine was it in?*

Salesperson: *I don't know. I'll ask my supervisor. (At this point, he turns away without covering the phone or putting the potential customer on hold, and asks supervisor.) She thinks it was a telemarketing magazine.*

Rebecca: *Oh, it was probably the press release in Inbound/Outbound.*

Salesperson: *So, why don't you have an 800 number?*

Rebecca: *(Struggling to continue to be polite) As I told you, we do.*

Salesperson: *Well, it's not through our company.*

Rebecca: *You're right. When we researched 800 numbers last summer we were told we couldn't get one from you on our type of line.*

Salesperson: *That's not right. Who told you that?*

Rebecca: *One of your representatives, six months ago.*

Salesperson: *Well, it wasn't me. So why isn't your 800 number in this ad?*

Rebecca: *(Almost losing patience) Because we didn't place the ad...*

What did this salesperson do wrong? What should he have done differently?

_____

_____

_____

Compare your answers with the author's suggested responses in the back of the book.

THE CASE OF THE ANNOYING AIRLINE AGENTS

Suzanne arrived at the airline counter to check in for the last flight of the evening to a small town called Kearney. It took four or five minutes for the young woman agent to help the two people ahead of Suzanne. Now it's Suzanne's turn. The agent busily begins typing into the computer.

Suzanne, after waiting a few minutes more: "It says 'check-in required' on my ticket."

Agent 1 (without looking up): "The other agent will be right with you," nodding toward a young male agent (Agent 2).

Agent 2 steps to Suzanne's left to ask a colleague something. Another passenger approaches him and he spends a few minutes helping him. The agent then turns to his computer to complete a task. Another passenger interrupts him.

Suzanne: *"Excuse me,"* she says, beginning to get impatient, *"I was next."*

Agent 2: *"I'll be with you in a moment, ma'am."*

Suzanne: *"I was next and you've already waited on two people who weren't in line."*

Agent 2: *"I'll be right there."*

Suzanne is beginning to fume.

Agent 1: *"Please be patient. This is our first day."*

"Great," Suzanne says sarcastically. "Let me share a little phrase that will help you a lot. It's 'Who was next?'"

Agent 2 now gives her a boarding pass. They don't say another word.

Suzanne's flight is announced. Agent 1 is collecting tickets, while chatting with another airline employee. Suzanne doesn't see anyone else boarding for the flight; maybe she's the only one going to this small town. There are three doors leading to the tarmac. None have flight numbers or destinations posted near them. She proceeds down the hallway toward the one she thought was her flight. She exits the open door into the night and proceeds down the flight of stairs to the tarmac. She looks up and notices the plane is darkened, and nearby is a pilot and airline employee.

CONTINUED

"Is this the plane to Kearney?" Suzanne asks, confused because the plane is dark.

"No," the employee answers, "You'll have to go back and ask the agent where the plane is."

Suzanne is now furious about the confusion and the airline's unresponsiveness. She meets another woman airline employee in the hallway. "Where's the plane to Kearney?" she seethes.

"It's down the other hallway," she says, motioning with her head.

"That woman agent is an incompetent twit," Suzanne hisses.

"No she's not. You shouldn't say that about her," the airline employee retorts.

What did each of the airline employees do wrong? How could they have handled the situation more positively?

_____

_____

_____

_____

_____

_____

Compare your answers with the author's suggested responses in the back of the book.

THE CASE OF THE FLIGHTY TRAVEL AGENT

Robert calls a national travel agency he's been using and asks for the manager. When he gets the manager, the conversation proceeds as follows:

Robert: *"Hello, I have had many problems getting the right ticket for a flight I'm leaving on tomorrow. I need someone who will take some responsibility."*

Manager: *"What's the problem?"*

Robert: *"Six weeks ago, Tomas sent me a ticket but the wrong date was on the ticket. I called immediately and was told by Bianca not to worry. I would be reticketed closer to my travel date."*

Manager: *"Bianca no longer works here."*

Robert: *"Yes, I was told that today when I called. Tomas had originally quoted me a $59 round-trip fare, the ticket showed $229, and Bianca said it should have been $179. She said she would send me new tickets last Friday. When I didn't receive them on Monday, I called again. Your office told me to call the San Francisco reservation center about any changes. I did. Louisa told me she would have a supervisor call me that day, Monday. No one did. Today is Wednesday. I'm flying tomorrow and don't have the correct tickets."*

Manager: *"When did you notice the problem?"*

Robert: *"Six weeks ago."*

Manager: *"And you're just now getting around to calling about it?"*

What did this manager do wrong? What should he have done differently?

_____

_____

_____

_

Compare your answers with the author's suggested responses in the back of the book.

THE CASE OF THE NERVY NEWSMAN

The sales rep of a local weekly business newspaper calls Bill, a customer. Here's part of the conversation:

Salesperson:	*"Do you plan to resubscribe?"*
Bill:	*"No, I don't."*
Salesperson:	*"Why not?"*
Bill:	*"Well, I decided the paper just wasn't worth $42 a year to me."*
Salesperson:	*"Are you kidding? What are you looking for that we don't have?"*
Bill:	*"I get more business information out of the daily paper."*
Salesperson:	*"I can't believe that. We have better business coverage than they do."*
Bill:	*"That's subjective."*
Salesperson:	*"No, it's not..."*

What did this salesperson do wrong? What should he have done differently?

_____

_____

_____

*Compare your answers with the author's suggested responses
in the back of the book.*

How Would You Handle the Situation?

Here are some situations you might encounter in your organization. They won't exactly match your situations, but they may be similar.

Write your responses in dialogue form—what you would actually say, not a description of the scene. Then ask a co-worker to role-play these scenes with you aloud and give each other feedback.

Example:

Customer: *"You have sent me someone else's canceled checks again. I have had it. I want to close my account right now."*

Bank Teller: *"I'm sorry about the mistake and I can understand your frustration. If you'll give me your account number, I'll get you the correct checks immediately. We'd hate to lose you as a customer."*

Now write your responses to the following complaints.

1. *"I have waited in line for 20 minutes. What takes you people so long?"*

   _____

   _____

2. *"You made a mistake again on my bill. My records say I owe $62.00 and your statement says I owe $323.50. I want you to fix it. Can't you people do anything right?"*

   _____

   _____

3. *"Your service has been totally unsatisfactory. You promised to deliver my software three weeks ago and I haven't heard from anyone since. I want it delivered today."*

   _____

   _____

=CONTINUED=

4. *"You have done this completely wrong. You are incompetent. I want to see your supervisor immediately so I can have you fired."*

_____

_____

5. *"Your manager has been letting me do it this way for years. Even though she isn't in today, why don't you just let me do it this way so I can stop wasting my time here?"*

_____

_____

6. Write a scenario that has happened to you that you felt uneasy dealing with. Write the customer's part as well as your own. Describe how you would respond now, after reading this book.

Past scenario:

_____

_____

_____

_____

_____

_____

How you would respond today:

_____

_____

_____

_____

_____

_____

_____

Compare your answers with the author's suggested responses in the back of the book.

After the Customer Has Gone

After the customer has left, you may want to take a few minutes for a time-out or a cool-down. You may need to compose and calm yourself.

Don't focus on what you did poorly. Don't reproach yourself for making mistakes. Instead, use this time to learn how you could handle the situation differently in the future. On the next page is an Incident Review form you can photocopy to review what happened.

INCIDENT REVIEW

1. What did I do well to calm this upset customer? (For example: called the customer by name, looked the customer in the eye, listened well, wanted to help, avoided interrupting.)

   _____

   _____

2. What could I have said that would have calmed the customer better or sooner?

   _____

   _____

3. What did I say that I don't want to say again?

   _____

   _____

4. What body language can I use to calm the upset customer better next time?

   _____

   _____

5. What body language do I want to work on eliminating so it doesn't escalate the upset?

   _____

   _____

6. What did I learn?

   _____

   _____

7. Think of two phrases that will help you remember both your value and your intentions. Two examples include the following:

   I am a valuable person.

   I am working on becoming the best I can be.

   _____

   _____

Don't Take It Personally or Bore Your Co-Workers

Don't Take It Personally

Even though the customer is actually upset at the organization, a policy, one of your co-workers, or himself, it is easy to feel as if the attack was personal. The customer is lashing out at whatever is near—in this case, you.

More often than not, his misfortune was not caused by you. You must remind yourself of this. If he says "You screwed up my order," he probably means "My order didn't arrive on time and you people are going to pay for this. Whoever did this is in big trouble, and since I don't know exactly who it is, you're going to hear my anger—perhaps you'll put things right."

Sometimes the mistake was your fault. We all make mistakes. It often disarms people if you admit it was your fault and apologize. But only do this if it really was your fault. If you have made the same mistake before, ask your supervisor how you can eliminate the error.

Don't Bore Your Co-workers

Some people say it helps to get over their own upset if they tell their co-workers about the incident. Ask yourself, "Was this a pleasant experience?" If not, why would you want to share an unpleasant experience with people you like? Will it make their day better? Will it make them happier? The answer is no, it won't make their day happier, so why burden them?

If there is something your co-workers can learn from your experience, then certainly you should share it. For example, you may have learned something about a customer's hot buttons, because you unknowingly set them off. This information is useful to your co-workers, so they won't get into the same hassle with this customer.

You may also want to ask your co-worker for advice. "What would you have done?" "What do you think I should have done?" "What should I do differently next time?" These questions can help you learn from the experience.

If you just want to get it off your chest, however, don't bother anyone else. Write out the story to yourself. This way, you can become your own advisor. Ask yourself what you could have done differently.

Review: What Did We Cover?

You now know why it's important to calm upset customers, why customers become upset, what you can do to reduce the chance of upset, how you can calm an upset customer, and what to do after he or she has left.

Why It Is Important to Calm Upset Customers

Customers are the reason you have a job. They deserve to have their complaints known and, when appropriate, to have something done about them.

You want them to complain because then they are more likely to be loyal to your business. When you respond to their concern promptly and professionally, they will keep coming back–happily.

Why Customers Get Upset

Sometimes you may do things that increase a customer's annoyance and escalate their anger. You can become aware of these behaviors and work at eliminating them.

What You Can Do to Avoid Upsets

Our personal presentation, body language, voice tone, and words all make a difference. If you pay attention to these, you can avoid escalating annoyance into anger.

Calming Upset Customers

You can listen caringly, sincerely, and fully to the customer's concern. You can defuse the customer's defensiveness by using Communication Helpers instead of Fight Starters.

What to Do After the Customer Has Gone

You can review the interaction to determine what you learned and what you could do differently next time.

What Managers Can Do

The next section provides some tips to help managers create an environment conducive to excellent customer service. Supervisors can be outstanding role models by continually showing the staff how customers should be treated. Two keys to building these skills are rewarding outstanding service behavior, and treating employees with the same respect customers should receive.

62

Tips for Managers

Guidelines for Managers

Managers don't always know how customers are being treated. When you aren't around or within earshot, how do you really know how your employees are responding to your customers? You don't. Therefore, ensure that your example of customer service lives on through your staff's interactions with customers.

As discussed in Part 2, some customers wouldn't have to be calmed were they not faced with annoyances to begin with. It is critical that you instill successful customer service concepts in your staff. Let's examine what managers can do to create an environment conducive to continual customer satisfaction.

Creating an Environment for Customer Satisfaction

Be a Role Model

You must give more than lip service to the concept of customer satisfaction—you must practice it visibly and frequently. Sending your staff to outside courses on customer satisfaction will be a waste of money if you don't model and reward good service.

Ask for Your Staff's Suggestions

Your employees often have good ideas to improve operations. However, some won't feel comfortable making suggestions unless asked.

Enact any ideas that make sense. Moreover, give credit for them. People resent it when someone else steals their thunder.

Solicit Customer Feedback

You have several inexpensive ways to get feedback:

➤ **Provide postage-paid return cards or surveys**

Make sure they're short and to the point. Include a place for the customer to write his or her name and telephone number so you can call to clarify any information.

➤ **Follow up with phone calls**

You could personally call five or 10 customers each week to check on service. Don't only call customers who you know love your company, but also some from whom you haven't heard in a while.

Observe service interactions and ask customers what changes they'd like to see.

Reward Good Customer Service Behavior

When a staff member does a good job, give her immediate feedback. Let her know what you noticed that showed good service. Be specific: "I was glad to hear you offer Mrs. Olsen help with her packages."

Become familiar with the concepts in this book so you can reinforce behavior that calms customers, and counsel your staff when they are behaving in ways that are annoying to customers.

Encourage Your Staff to Use Their Initiative

Give your staff the authority to act on the customer's behalf. Set a guideline for how much money they can spend to resolve an issue without calling in a supervisor. Increase the amount as your trust in their judgment increases. This gives them confidence, and allows the customer's problem to be handled immediately.

In a recent article in *Frequent Flyer,* Paul Auger, vice-president of marketing for an airline, says:

"Employees now have the ability to resolve problems—whatever the problem is—without saying that our policy is 'Write a letter to the president.' For example, we tell our personnel we're not going to punish them for giving away a free ticket. We counsel them if we feel they're being overzealous. But as long as they feel they're doing it on behalf of the customer, the worst that can happen is that we say, 'Gee, did you really have to go that far?'"

Don't Talk Negatively About Customers

Saying "Mrs. Hanson is such a pain in the neck," teaches nothing. But saying "Mrs. Hanson is very detail-oriented, so make sure to check her invoices carefully before you send them out," explains your concern and what to do about it.

Know When to Fire a Customer

If a customer continually upsets your staff for trivial reasons, you may need to invite the customer to use someone else's services. "Mr. Pratt, it seems that we cannot meet your expectations. Perhaps another vendor could meet your standards." Of course, if your organization is a utility, public agency, or government office, this is not an option for you.

Using This Book for a Staff Meeting

Using this workbook in a staff meeting can help to interest your staff in learning techniques for dealing with customers.

Hand out the books a week or two before your next staff meeting, telling everyone that the topic of the next meeting will be how to calm upset customers.

Each employee is responsible for reading the book, completing the exercises, and coming up with ideas on how to adapt the concepts to your group's situations.

When you lead the meeting, become a facilitator, not a dictator. Draw out your staff by asking them open-ended questions about the situations and concepts. Avoid lecturing. Although you are the boss, you will turn everyone off if you tell them that the way you handle people is the right and only way.

Some questions you can use to begin the discussion include the following:

"Suzanne, share with us your response to question four on page 28 in the 'Watch Your Words' practice. Would you elaborate on why you think it's important never to treat a customer the way the staff did in this example?"

"Blake, how do you think we could adapt _____ here?"

"What ideas do you have for eliminating things that could annoy our customers?"

Have regular discussions at staff meetings about customer service. Provide examples of good customer-service behavior, as well as problems that may need correcting (don't embarrass anyone). Continually make your concerns and attitude known.

Teach Your Staff How to Learn from Negative Experiences

Use the questions in the Incident Review sheet in Part 4:

➤   What did you do well?

➤   What would you do differently next time?

➤   What could you do to prevent this from happening again?

➤   What did you learn?

Evaluate Customer Satisfaction Performance

Be clear about the minimum levels of customer service you expect. Be specific. For example:

➤   Telephones to be answered within two rings

➤   All walk-in visitors greeted within 30 seconds

➤   Phone calls returned within four hours

➤   Upbeat and helpful behavior

➤   Smile when greeting customers

Let staff members know that their behavior in these areas will be included in their performance evaluation.

When Managers Calm Upset Customers

The upset customer may be passed to you if your employee can't handle the situation, or if the customer insists on seeing you.

Not only is there an urgent need to calm this customer, your staff are also listening and watching to see how you handle the situation. Remember that you are a role model.

Often, the customer will seem calmer and more rational with you than with your staff because you are perceived as having more authority to do something about the problem.

On the other hand, your staff may have done something to escalate the customer's anger. You should be able to handle any situation if you use the guidelines in this book.

When You Blow It

If you do or say something that annoys the customer further, and you realize your error in retrospect, discuss it at a staff meeting. Explain what you did wrong, and either ask the group to suggest a better response or explain what you think you should have said or done.

A leader who is willing to admit errors, discuss them, and strategize corrections is a leader who will be respected. Don't be afraid of being vulnerable in front of your staff. If you talk about your mistakes and act to correct them, you will have the respect of your employees.

Managing Upset Employees

In addition to stepping in when necessary to calm upset customers yourself, one of your management responsibilities is to help employees through these experiences. At times, you may need to stand up for the employee and support him during an incident. You should also support the employee afterwards, helping him regain composure and get back on a positive footing. You can also help your entire staff learn from each incident and provide a safe environment for learning from one another.

Part 1: During the Incident

Whether she's right or wrong, it's important that you not make your employee look foolish or incompetent.

If she was right in what she told the customer, say so.

"Mrs. Wong, I'm sorry to tell you that your Blue Bird phone service allows you to receive discounts only on calls made inside your area code between noon and 2 P.M. As Nancy explained, this is the reason for the calls at 2:08 and 3:32 being charged at the full rate."

If only you can make an exception to the policy your employee stated, tell the customer so. Emphasize that the employee was doing her job well.

If the employee was wrong, explain that there must have been a misinterpretation of policy. Emphasize his value in front of the customer.

"Yes, Mr. Jones, you are right that you shouldn't be charged for cashiers' checks on your Senior Special account. Obviously, there was a misunderstanding about this. Bill is one of our finest tellers, so I'm sure it was an oversight. At our next staff meeting, I'll remind all our tellers. I'm sorry for your inconvenience. Of course, we'll waive the fee for your cashier's check. Is there anything else we can do for you today?"

Part 2: After the Customer Has Left

Your employee may be shaken, angry, or on the verge of tears. Allow her to retain self-respect and composure in front of her peers and the other customers. Let her take a 10-minute break so she can go to the lounge, restroom, or other quiet place to compose herself.

If at all possible, accompany her and talk to her about the exchange, listen to her vent her anger, and reinforce your support of her actions. When she's calm enough, discuss with her how she might handle the situation differently next time. (If she's very upset, postpone the discussion until another time.) Solicit her ideas before telling her yours. The last thing she needs right now is a lecture.

Part 3: Debriefing the Rest of the Staff

If the rest of the staff heard or saw the incident, it may be appropriate to discuss the scene with them. If it was a serious or physical altercation, debrief them as soon as possible, preferably at the close of that business day or shift. If it was less serious, discuss it at the next staff meeting. Be sure to discuss it with the involved employee beforehand, and check whether sharing it with others would be okay with him or her.

Recap what happened, then focus the discussion on what can be learned: what worked to help calm this customer, and what might be tried differently next time. Don't make negative remarks about the customer's behavior or character.

Customer Satisfaction

Customer satisfaction is essential to an organization's survival. Instill the value of this with your staff, recognize their commendable behavior, and teach them to think on behalf of the customer—and you'll have an organization your customers will keep coming back to.

Assure customer satisfaction and you'll be a winner.

A P P E N D I X

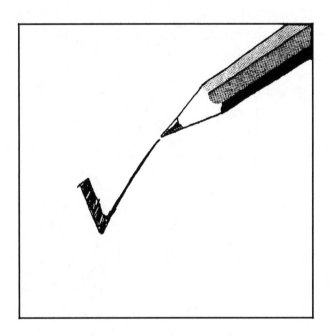

Author's Suggested Responses

Watch Your Words (pages 28–31)

The following are the author's suggested responses to the previous situations.

1. This response is negative. Rephrase it as a positive response:

   "Yes, I'd be glad to hold it until closing time tonight, which is 6:00."

2. Again, this is negative. It assumes that the customer doesn't qualify.

   Rephrase it without the negative assumption:

   "I'd be delighted to add you to the list. This list is for customers who meet the qualification of having spent $1,000 with us this year. Does that qualification fit you?"

3. This response will make the customer feel embarrassed, and probably angry. Rephrase it to make it less personal:

   "I'm sorry for the delay. It seems that the form was not completed correctly. I'll help you put it right."

4. It doesn't answer the question. Also, it sounds like an order. Rephrase it to invite the customer to visit the Accessories Department, instead of saying he has to:

   "Yes, we do carry mittens. There's a wide selection in our Accessories Department, which is at the top of those stairs."

5. This response is not very helpful. Rephrase it to offer some assistance to the customer:

   "Let me check for you."

6. This is a flip response to a serious question. Rephrase it to give the information she asked for:

   "You can call her during her office hours, Mondays, Wednesdays, and Fridays, between 2:00 and 4:00, at 555-1212, or drop in on her during those times in Room 733, or put a note in her mailbox in Room 345. Let me write that down for you."

7. Tell the customer what you can do, not what you can't do.

   "I'm sorry, we've closed out for the day. I'd be glad to take the information and change it first thing in the morning."

8. This is insulting to the customer, and assumes she didn't read the manual. Even if she did read the manual, she may need further clarification.

> *"I'm not sure. Please tell me what it's doing and not doing and we'll troubleshoot together."*

9. Not very helpful, is it? Give the information asked for:

> *"Let me look that up for you. I'll be just another moment."*

10. The staff person is calling the customer a liar. Rephrase it without the accusation:

> *"I'm sorry for the confusion. Let me pull your record so we can see what happened and fix it. What's your last name, please?"*

11. Not very helpful, is it? Give the information asked for:

> *"It's down this hall, then take a left and you'll see it straight ahead."*

12. Don't tell your customer you have other customer problems. It isn't relevant to their concern about their order, and it implies that customer problems are common in your organization. This may make them take their business elsewhere because they have lost confidence in your business. A better response is:

> *"Let me look into that for you."*

13. Customers don't want to hear "It's policy." Explain how this policy is a benefit to the customer.

> *"We ask for two identifications for your protection. I'm sure many other bank personnel know you, Mr. Perez. I'm new here so I want to make sure I'm not giving your money to someone who says he's you but isn't."*

14. Answer the question without telling the customer what she has to do:

> *"Please tell me about it and I'll see what I can do to straighten it out."*

15. This is not a helpful response. It's annoying.

> *"Let me walk you through it and point out the steps in the manual."*

16. Never make the customer call back. It's not their problem or fault that the computer is down.

> *"I'll be glad to check that for you and call you back as soon as our computer is running again."*

The Case of the Surly Salesperson *(page 50)*

Let's analyze the conversation and discuss key areas of conflict.

He was blunt. The salesperson should have considered the words he used and how they can affect the customer. When the salesperson initially confronted Rebecca with "Why don't you have an 800 number?" she became annoyed. He could have said: "Congratulations on your new video, 'Calming Upset Customers.' This is Larry Smith from The Best Long Distance Telephone Company. I noticed there wasn't an 800 number listed in the announcement. I thought one would help increase your orders. Do you currently have an 800 number?"

Instead, he assumed Rebecca didn't have an 800 number. He also assumed she had placed an ad, when actually it was a press release, which meant she had no control over which information the magazine chose to publish.

When you need clarification, ask questions politely, and with sincere interest. Don't be confrontational with your questions. Modify blunt questions with "May I ask," "Would you share with me," or "By the way."

He was argumentative. He demanded to know who in his company had misinformed Rebecca although she told him it had been over six months since she'd received the information.

If you disagree with something, don't respond with "That's not true." Instead, try, "I don't understand how that could have happened. Tell me more."

Twice he didn't listen to the answers to his questions and asked them again. Few things annoy people more than repeating answers to the same questions. If you don't remember what someone said, acknowledge it: "I'm sorry, I blanked out a moment. Would you tell me again why your 800 number isn't in this announcement?" That shows you're human and polite.

His tone of voice sounded impatient and frustrated at not making the sale. No wonder he was frustrated; because he wasn't listening to himself or Rebecca, he had no idea why he wasn't getting anywhere.

The Case of the Annoying Airline Agents (pages 51–52)

Agent 1 didn't acknowledge Suzanne when she was done with the previous customer. She could have said pleasantly "Let me just finish this gentleman's reservation and I'll be right with you."

Agent 2 also could have acknowledged Suzanne with an "I'll be just a second" to Suzanne. When the other passenger approached him he should have said, "Let me help this woman and I'll be right with you." Or, "I'll be glad to help you with that as soon as I'm done with this customer." He helped other passengers twice before helping Suzanne, who was next in line.

Agent 1 was so busy chatting with her co-worker she didn't make sure Suzanne was going in the right direction. This leads to a potentially dangerous situation with Suzanne walking out onto the tarmac with no guidance.

The third airline employee should not have argued with Suzanne (and yes, Suzanne should not have called the other agent a twit). The third employee could have defused the situation by asking what was wrong and then escorting Suzanne to the correct door.

The Case of the Flighty Travel Agent (page 53)

The manager's responses didn't indicate a sincere attempt to help solve the problem. It didn't matter that Bianca no longer worked there. His response suggested he didn't want to take responsibility for what she had said because she was no longer an employee.

Nor did it matter how long ago the problem was noticed, as Robert had already explained the sequence of events. The manager should have focused on fixing the problem, not on inconsequential details that Robert had already covered.

The final blow was when he seemed to blame Robert for the problem by saying, "And you're just now getting around to calling about it?" Robert had been tracking the problem, and was told it would be taken care of by various employees.

The Case of the Nervy Newsman (page 54)

The salesperson was confrontational with his questions. Instead of "Why not?" a gentler question like "Really? Help me understand why" would have elicited a more informational response.

His reaction to the reason Bill wasn't resubscribing was also confrontational. "Are you kidding?" implies that Bill is a fool for not seeing the value of the paper.

Then he gets argumentative when Bill explains that he likes the business coverage in the local paper better. He's arguing with Bill's opinion. There's no possibility for a sale with this rep.

If you remember only three things:

    1. Listen completely

    2. Speak respectfully

    3. Focus on positive actions

How Would You Handle the Situation? (pages 55–56)

1. *"I can understand how you'd be upset. You've waited a long time. I'll help you get through your transaction quickly. How can I help you now?"*

2. *"I'm sorry your account doesn't balance. Let me research your account transactions and see what went wrong so we can make sure it doesn't happen again. May I have your account number, please?"*

3. *"I can understand why you'd be upset. I would be too. I'm sorry your software hasn't been delivered. Let me look into what went wrong. Do you have the order number and date? Would you like to wait while I research this, or would you prefer I get back to you within the hour?"*

4. *"I'm sorry you are dissatisfied with my service. Please tell me specifically what wasn't right so I can correct it. And I'll get Mrs. Hall, my supervisor, for you."*

5. *"I can understand why you feel this procedure is a waste of time. I'm sorry, I don't have the authority to complete this transaction differently—only the manager does. When she comes back, I will check to see if I can handle your account differently next time you come in. I'm sorry for the inconvenience today."*

Additional Reading

Barlow, Janelle and Claus Moeller. *A Complaint Is a Gift*. San Francisco: Berrett-Koehler, 1996.

Bonet, Diana. *The Business of Listening*. Boston, MA: Thomson Learning/Course Technology, 2001.

Chapman, Elwood N. and Wil McKnight. *Attitude: Your Most Priceless Possession*. Boston, MA: Thomson Learning/Course Technology, 2002.

Charles, C. Leslie. *Why Is Everyone So Cranky?* New York: Hyperion, 1999.

Finch, Lloyd. *Telephone Courtesy and Customer Service*. Boston, MA: Thomson Learning/Course Technology, 2000.

Kindler, Herbert S. *Managing Disagreement Constructively, Revised Edition*. Boston, MA: Thomson Learning/Course Technology, 1996.

Martin, William B. *Quality Customer Service, Fourth Edition*. Boston, MA: Thomson Learning/Course Technology, 2001.

Minor, Marianne. *Preventing Workplace Violence*. Boston, MA: Thomson Learning/Course Technology, 1995.

Morgan, Rebecca L. *Life's Lessons: Insights and Information for a Richer Life*. Morgan Seminar Group, 1997.

Stiel, Holly. *Thank You Very Much: A Book for Anyone Who Has Ever Said, "May I help you?"* Berkeley, CA: Ten Speed Press, 1995.

Zemke, Ron and John Woods, eds. *Best Practices in Customer Service*. New York: AMACOM, 1999.

Now Available From

THOMSON ™

COURSE TECHNOLOGY

Books•Videos•CD-ROMs•Computer-Based Training Products

If you enjoyed this book, we have great news for you. There are over 200 books available in the ***Crisp Fifty-Minute™ Series***.
For more information contact

Course Technology
25 Thomson Place
Boston, MA 02210
1-800-442-7477
www.courseilt.com

Subject Areas Include:

Management
Human Resources
Communication Skills
Personal Development
Sales/Marketing
Finance
Coaching and Mentoring
Customer Service/Quality
Small Business and Entrepreneurship
Training
Life Planning
Writing

Calming Upset Customers